DATE DUE

OCT 2 1 2010	

Yellow Umbrella Books are published by Red Brick Learning
7825 Telegraph Road, Bloomington, Minnesota 55438
http://www.redbricklearning.com

Library of Congress Cataloging-in-Publication Data
Catala, Ellen.
 Who keeps us safe?/by Ellen Catala.
 p. cm.
 Summary: "Simple text and photos present many people in the community
that work to keep others safe"—Provided by publisher.
 Includes index.
 ISBN-13: 978-0-7368-5984-4 (hardcover)
 ISBN-10: 0-7368-5984-5 (hardcover)
 ISBN 0-7368-1720-4 (softcover)
 1. Police—Juvenile literature. 2. Fire fighters—Juvenile literature. 3. Physicians—
Juvenile literature. 4. Teachers—Juvenile literature. 5. Family—Juvenile literature.
I. Title.
HV7922.C38 2006
363.1—dc22   2005025748

Written by Ellen Catala
Developed by Raindrop Publishing

Editorial Director: Mary Lindeen
Editor: Jennifer VanVoorst
Photo Researcher: Wanda Winch
Conversion Assistants: Jenny Marks, Laura Manthe

Photo Credits
Cover: Gary Sundermeyer/Capstone Press; Title Page: Richard Hutchings/Corbis;
Page 4: Tim Wright/Corbis; Page 6: Table Mesa Productions/Index Stock; Page 8:
Grantpix/Index Stock; Page 10: Reed Kaestner/Corbis; Page 12: Frank Siteman/Index
Stock; Page 14: PhotoDisc; Page 16: Gary Sundermeyer/Capstone Press

1 2 3 4 5 6 11 10 09 08 07 06

Who Keeps Us Safe?

by Ellen Catala

Yellow
Umbrella
Books
for early readers

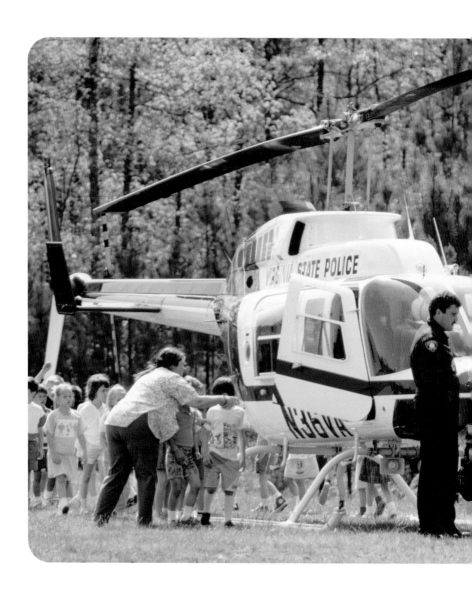

Who keeps us safe?

Police officers keep us safe.

Firefighters keep us safe.

Doctors keep us safe.

Teachers keep us safe.

Families keep us safe.

We are safe.

Index